♥ Love, Life,

LOVE, LIFE, AND CHOCOLATE CHIP COOKIES

by

Donna Lagorio Montgomery

*To Pat!
Love life!
Donna Montgomery*

♥ LOVE, LIFE, AND CHOCOLATE CHIP COOKIES ♥

A St. John's Book/ Spring 1995

All rights reserved.
Copyright © 1995 by Donna L. Montgomery

No part of this book may be reproduced or transmitted in any form or by any means, electronic or mechanical, including information storage and retrieval systems, without permission in writing from the publisher, except by a reviewer who may quote brief passages in a review.

Published by
St. John's Publishing, Inc.,
6824 Oaklawn Avenue, Edina, Minnesota, 55435.

ISBN 0-938577-10-7

First Edition 0 9 8 7 6 5 4 3 2 1

♥ Love, Life, and Chocolate Chip Cookies ♥

DEDICATION

Moms and dads, as well as everyone else, need encouragement. Consider yourselves hugged!

♥ Love, Life, and Chocolate Chip Cookies ♥

1 ♥ Chocolate chip cookies are keys to a child's heart, no matter what the child's age.

2 ♥ We renew our wonder of nature's beauty through the eyes of children.

3 ♥ Mothers are the family's yeast, raising its ingredients to maximum potential.

♥ Love, Life, and Chocolate Chip Cookies ♥

4 ♥ Treat a child; feed your soul.

5 ♥ Praise the child and reinforce the adult.

6 ♥ Harm the child; destroy the adult.

7 ♥ Children given recognition at home choose good peer groups.

♥ Love, Life, and Chocolate Chip Cookies ♥

8 ♥ Don't worry about being a burden to your children, it didn't bother them being a burden to you.

9 ♥ Anger comes and goes, but true love is forever.

10 ♥ Women are each other's best friends and worst enemies, sometimes concurrently.

♥ LOVE, LIFE, AND CHOCOLATE CHIP COOKIES ♥

11 ♥ Can you look at the complexity and design of the human body and doubt the existence of God?

12 ♥ Sometimes those starved for love become fools for attention.

13 ♥ Be cheerleaders for each other.

♥ Love, Life, and Chocolate Chip Cookies ♥

20 ♥ Home is where we reveal our true selves and find out our families love us anyway.

21 ♥ I'll never be too busy to listen when I'm needed.

22 ♥ Death is rude, never asking if we're ready, but just barging in without so much as an "excuse me" or "I'm extremely sorry."

♥ Love, Life, and Chocolate Chip Cookies ♥

23 ♥ Marriage is like a merry-go-round ride that keeps going around in circles, with ups and downs, and in the end, leaves a person wanting more or wanting out.

24 ♥ What's better than curling up with a good book in front of a roaring fireplace and watching the first thick snow flakes of winter float softly to the ground?

25 ♥ Love takes many forms, mostly unspoken.

26 ♥ Birthing an idea is like birthing a child: both arrive on their own time schedule.

♥ Love, Life, and Chocolate Chip Cookies ♥

27 ♥ Beauty is best when it comes from inside.

28 ♥ The true measure of parents' effectiveness is whether they taught their children to be independent.

29 ♥ Be thoughtful when giving advice, since you'll also be expected to take it.

30 ♥ Flowers are the smile in God's eyes.

31 ♥ Hug a child; it enriches the giver and receiver.

32 ♥ Life is service.

33 ♥ Rewards aren't always of this earth.

♥ Love, Life, and Chocolate Chip Cookies ♥

34 ♥ Each person is God personified.

♥ Love, Life, and Chocolate Chip Cookies ♥

35 ♥ Kindnesses received free my spirit and give me a hint of what perfect happiness must feel like.

36 ♥ Knowing I'm loved and cared for makes me feel special.

37 ♥ I give my love to you freely.

♥ Love, Life, and Chocolate Chip Cookies ♥

38 ♥ Recognition is a lot like love; the more it's shared, the more it grows.

39 ♥ If they're good, say the words when you think them.

40 ♥ Recognize people each day for trying their best, thinking of others, or doing an unselfish act.

♥ Love, Life, and Chocolate Chip Cookies ♥

41 ♥ Thank you for listening to my problems and never trying to solve them.

42 ♥ A best friend's bond is as strong as family and very special.

43 ♥ Our dreams have changed, my husband. How have we done? Tell me, and I'll tell you.

♥ Love, Life, and Chocolate Chip Cookies ♥

44 ♥ Let's celebrate together, my friend, while there's still time.

45 ♥ Have I told my children how deeply they're loved, and how lovable they are?

46 ♥ Children don't need lessons pounded into them by spanking.

♥ Love, Life, and Chocolate Chip Cookies ♥

47 ♥ Life's lessons often come hard and fast, but tempered with humor and good spirit, nothing can get the best of us.

48 ♥ The empty nest syndrome is here at last; whoever said the years go fast?

49 ♥ Good listeners grow in wisdom.

♥ Love, Life, and Chocolate Chip Cookies ♥

50 ♥ My valentine forever, that's what you'll always be.

51 ♥ We should strive to say nothing at the very best times.

52 ♥ May you be blessed with a friend just like yourself.

♥ LOVE, LIFE, AND CHOCOLATE CHIP COOKIES ♥

53. ♥ If you fight for justice you're a winner, no matter the outcome.

54 ♥ We need good friends to share the child in us.

55 ♥ Believe in yourself, then you'll be able to believe in others.

♥ Love, Life, and Chocolate Chip Cookies ♥

56 ♥ Kind words leave a joyful memory; cruel words nullify them forever.

♥ Love, Life, and Chocolate Chip Cookies ♥

57 ♥ When my time comes, may I exit with laughter and a tear in my eye.

58 ♥ At the end of each day I pray I've made more wise choices than foolish ones, spreading a little joy along the way.

59 ♥ Vacations usually end with mixed feelings of fun remembered and home missed.

♥ Love, Life, and Chocolate Chip Cookies ♥

60 ♥ Minds and bodies need rejuvenation.

61 ♥ Love grows when we give it away.

62 ♥ Hugs are recyclable.

♥ Love, Life, and Chocolate Chip Cookies ♥

63 ♥ Before a child enters school, character is formed.

64 ♥ Children are born with clean slates; parents must be careful what they write on them.

65 ♥ Art takes many forms that surround us daily; sometimes we forget to look.

♥ Love, Life, and Chocolate Chip Cookies ♥

66 ♥ Even the tiniest flower on the tiniest weed is always consistant in color, shape, and size. Isn't that amazing? Teach your children to be amazed.

67 ♥ What we feel inside is more important than what we feel outside.

♥ Love, Life, and Chocolate Chip Cookies ♥

68 ♥ Always speak to young children at their eye level.

69 ♥ If we don't have compassion, how can we give it?

70 ♥ When the time comes for accounting to another, blessings on you magician mother.

♥ Love, Life, and Chocolate Chip Cookies ♥

71 ♥ If we have a choice to clean house or take a walk with our children, remember, work can be done another day, but moments with children can never be captured again.

72 ♥ Mothers have a unique partnership with God in the creation of life: they're vessels entrusted to carry His creation and to care for His child.

♥ Love, Life, and Chocolate Chip Cookies ♥

73 ♥ Motherhood is a condition acquired most of the time with no previous knowledge, education, training, or desire.

74 ♥ Motherhood is the most important, difficult, rewarding, depressing, and exhilarating job a woman can have.

♥ LOVE, LIFE, AND CHOCOLATE CHIP COOKIES ♥

75 ♥ The feeling when a newborn is first placed in mother's arms will always be remembered; responsibility takes on new meaning, changing life for everyone forever.

76 ♥ From beautiful, innocent, toddling twos to emotional, hair-trigger teens, life becomes a rollercoaster of peaks and valleys.

♥ Love, Life, and Chocolate Chip Cookies ♥

77 ♥ Sometimes in the hurry of meeting a family's physical needs, emotional needs of everyone are neglected. Relax! Take a break!

78 ♥ Mothers, may you ride in a golden chariot in the carpool to heaven.

79 ♥ Ah, hindsight. If only parents could have it when dealing in foresight!

♥ Love, Life, and Chocolate Chip Cookies ♥

80 ♥ Dads are now allowed to show tender emotions that somehow add to their strength rather than diminish it, making everyone winners.

81 ♥ I hate to say, "I told you so!" but you know that I did. You always were the greatest kid, and I'm happy that I told you so.

82 ♥ With our own children we must be careful not to expect the "firsts" to come sooner and oftener than they do for other people's children.

83 ♥ When children start school, parents sometimes set unrealistic goals, watching for signs of genius and looking at how children are different, rather than how they're the same.

84 ♥ Some parents are afraid to have their children touched by life's problems, so they make them their own and try to solve them for their children.

85 ♥ My kitchen curtain rises daily on the neighborhood theater; the play is on at my convenience.

♥ LOVE, LIFE, AND CHOCOLATE CHIP COOKIES ♥

86 ♥ Family is wonderful, husbands are wonderful, but every woman needs other women.

87 ♥ At times a mother feels like everyone's servant with no identity of her own, but remember, "the greatest among you is the servant of all."

♥ Love, Life, and Chocolate Chip Cookies ♥

88 ♥ It's not easy to be a mother, and it's extremely difficult to be a good one.

89 ♥ Mothers and fathers, as much as anyone, need encouragement.

90 ♥ We should take time to carefully observe the universe, and teach our children to be good observers, too.

91 ♥ Year after year, nature's seasons unfold their splendor before us, but we seem to miss the beauty of their comings and goings.

92 ♥ Isn't it amazing that with millions of cells in our bodies, they each end up in the right place at birth?

♥ Love, Life, and Chocolate Chip Cookies ♥

93 ♥ The order and consistency in nature should never cease to amaze us.

94 ♥ Think of everything you see in nature and be awed by it; then teach your children to be awed by it.

95 ♥ We need to juggle listening and speaking, using wisdom in deciding when to use each.

♥ LOVE, LIFE, AND CHOCOLATE CHIP COOKIES ♥

96 ♥ In view of the remarkable intelligence reflected in nature's designs, is it really possible we could have just happened to exist?

97 ♥ The miracle of the human body is a gift to everyone; children should be taught to appreciate it and use it wisely.

♥ Love, Life, and Chocolate Chip Cookies ♥

98 ♥ Why does it take us so long to become good listeners?

99 ♥ Help us resist preaching about the good old days, standing in judgment, or giving unwanted advice.

100 ♥ Wisdom can turn the complicated into brilliant simplicity.

♥ Love, Life, and Chocolate Chip Cookies ♥

101 ♥ It usually takes a lifetime to get up to speed in wisdom.

102 ♥ Remember what a special gift you are to so many people.

103 ♥ Every person has the capability to make love happen, starting in their own home.

♥ LOVE, LIFE, AND CHOCOLATE CHIP COOKIES ♥

104 ♥ Tradition is a quiet presence in each life.

105 ♥ Children quite often start a tradition based on a happy memory they want to repeat.

106 ♥ One person's tradition is not anothers.

107 ♥ Old-timers remember the smells and tastes of their youth, and feelings of fleeting moments.

108 ♥ If we only knew with foresight what we discover in hindsight, memories might all be happy ones.

♥ Love, Life, and Chocolate Chip Cookies ♥

109 ♥ My child now feeds me and holds me in loving arms; my life is full circle.

110 ♥ Best friends can be closer than brothers and sisters, sharing secrets no one else need ever know.

111 ♥ Dear friend, I like it when you're in my corner.

♥ LOVE, LIFE, AND CHOCOLATE CHIP COOKIES ♥

112 ♥ Friends like you happen so seldom in a lifetime, you deserve to be nurtured and loved for all the joy you spread so unselfishly.

113 ♥ You're fun, positive, uplifting, and know when to laugh me out of a bad mood or sit next to me and let me talk.

114 ♥ You're as comfortable as my favorite sweatshirt and tennis shoes, and as comforting as a cup of hot chocolate in cold hands on a winter's day.

♥ Love, Life, and Chocolate Chip Cookies ♥

115 ♥ I don't need to put on any airs for you, nor you for me.

116 ♥ You're perfect just the way you are, and I'm so glad you let me be your friend.

117 ♥ Life is short and memory long; to make you unhappy is always wrong.

♥ LOVE, LIFE, AND CHOCOLATE CHIP COOKIES ♥

118 ♥ Please forgive my thoughtless ways; I'll try to give you happier days.

119 ♥ I'm sorry that I hurt your heart; I didn't have the right.

120 ♥ Woman to woman, it's fun to talk, as we visit over coffee or go for a walk.

121 ♥ We labor for family out of love and tradition; we labor for ourselves to better our condition.

122 ♥ I need to know when the chips are down, that good friends are in the wings, nonjudgmentally telling me things...like what a good friend I've been, loyal and true, and how I have helped you whenever you're blue.

♥ Love, Life, and Chocolate Chip Cookies ♥

123 ♥ Days are never boring as long as we make time to play together.

124 ♥ I wake up and see your familiar face across the pillow and know all is right with the world.

125 ♥ Growing into life together brings our love full circle, sometimes daily.

♥ Love, Life, and Chocolate Chip Cookies ♥

126 ♥ With the sweetness of maturity comes bountiful fruit ripe for enjoyment.

127 ♥ Age tempers our relationships, making them more comfortable and routine.

128 ♥ Golden years are here; we have the right to celebrate our jobs well done.

♥ Love, Life, and Chocolate Chip Cookies ♥

129 ♥ Women need to relish their womanhood, remember their childhood, laugh, and cry.

130 ♥ Faithful friend, heart of my heart, tell me, has life been good to you?

131 ♥ Children are sweet innocence, laughter, and mischief rolled into ring around the rosies and downright joy.

132 ♥ As we mature in wisdom, we realize wealth isn't material, but comes in relationships.

133 ♥ My children, now it's your turn to watch your dear little children discover all that you know, and more.

134 ♥ Our friendship never needs explanations or gives demands, but conforms to each other's likes and dislikes, while retaining our individuality.

135 ♥ Newly plowed farm fields in the spring remind us of God's continuing trust in the human beings he created.

♥ Love, Life, and Chocolate Chip Cookies ♥

136 ♥ I praise God for every day that's given with no strings.

137 ♥ No matter how my days are filled, may I never say I'm "too busy" to family or a friend in need.

138 ♥ I come; I leave my mark. How quickly the evidence of my passage will be erased.

♥ Love, Life, and Chocolate Chip Cookies ♥

139 ♥ My family is the greatest gift,
    a miracle without equal;
    yet God promised with all this,
    the best will be life's sequel.

♥ Love, Life, and Chocolate Chip Cookies ♥

140 ♥ If refrigerators could talk, they'd certainly have a lot to say.

141 ♥ Kindness put upon life's table comes right back to us.

142 ♥ Time spent with children in their youth pays dividends when they enter adulthood armed with family values learned at home.

♥ Love, Life, and Chocolate Chip Cookies ♥

143 ♥ When I give of myself or worldly goods, I get much more in return.

144 ♥ If we could choose our problems, what would they be? The ones we already have?

145 ♥ Our mind's eye is gentler than the others.

146 ♥ I'm trying to never say "I should have."

♥ Love, Life, and Chocolate Chip Cookies ♥

147 ♥ First we lose grandparents, then parents, and now it's us.

148 ♥ How exciting it is to be exuberant with wild abandon at the humble thought of all life's simple, inexpensive pleasures.

149 ♥ May we never have to say, "I should have," because we always did.

♥ LOVE, LIFE, AND CHOCOLATE CHIP COOKIES ♥

150 ♥ There may be a whole world "out there," but there's also a whole world inside the home as well, which we experience only briefly, so enjoy!

151 ♥ Mothers are tough; they've been through the fire, surviving kids both loving and hating them.

152 ♥ No other group in the world is so forgiving, or has been asked to forgive so much, over and over, as mothers.

153 ♥ Mothers have mothers of their own, and now, as mothers themselves, possess a unique perspective.

♥ Love, Life, and Chocolate Chip Cookies ♥

154 ♥ Tell moms anything, they won't be shocked. Reject them and they'll come back. The worst thing would be to ignore them. Mothers, as much as anyone, need recognition.

155 ♥ A life-lover rejoices in the spring of the year, and becomes nostalgic in the fall.

♥ Love, Life, and Chocolate Chip Cookies ♥

156 ♥ Our free will is tempered by conscience, but we often use one and ignore the other.

♥ Love, Life, and Chocolate Chip Cookies ♥

157 ♥ We should take time to carefully observe nature, so we can teach our children to be good observers.

158 ♥ Day after day, month after month, year after year, nature's seasons unfold their splendors before us, but we seem to miss the beauty of their comings and goings.

♥ Love, Life, and Chocolate Chip Cookies ♥

159 ♥ Parents need to have a sense of humor and learn to laugh at themselves.

160 ♥ You can't look at life's situations with a sense of humor and remain a pessimist.

161 ♥ Nature plays no favorites. The wonders and miracles of the human body and the universe are gifts to all, not just an elite few.

162 ♥ Children should be taught to appreciate the precious gift of their body and how to use it with respect and dignity.

163 ♥ Many children have become little more than machines, overloaded with fuel and kept running continuously from home, to school, to day care center, and back again.

♥ Love, Life, and Chocolate Chip Cookies ♥

164 ♥ There's time enough in life to do everything we want to do, just not all at the same time.

165 ♥ When a baby communicates in the only way babies can, by crying, be ready to assume something is wrong, then offer all the comfort you can.

166 ♥ Sometimes, lack of good day care for children has burdened some moms with so much guilt, the money they earn to improve their quality of life is spent on psychologists to get rid of the guilt destroying a family's quality of life.

167 ♥ Looking back through picture albums at happy, growing children, is enough to bring tears to a mom's eyes, and usually does.

168 ♥ The best part of any event is usually the anticipation.

169 ♥ People need something pleasant to look forward to, rather than past hurts on which to brood.

170 ♥ Surprise parties can be fun once or twice in a lifetime, but not too often, because they deprive us of anticipation, which is one of the best parts of a party.

171 ♥ If you plan on baking cookies or cooking a favorite meal for supper, tell kids and mate about it in the morning so they can enjoy anticipating it all day.

172 ♥ Spanking vents the anger of the spanker, but does nothing to solve the problem of the "spankee."

♥ LOVE, LIFE, AND CHOCOLATE CHIP COOKIES ♥

173 ♥ Anticipation is worth planning.

♥ LOVE, LIFE, AND CHOCOLATE CHIP COOKIES ♥

174 ♥ The rewards of a mother's creativity will come back to her in many surprising ways through her children, and her children someday will pay her the ultimate compliment: imitation.

♥ Love, Life, and Chocolate Chip Cookies ♥

175 ♥ If you must give a negative reply, try putting a positive twist to it. Example: "Mom, can I have a piece of candy?" Answer: "Yes, right after dinner," rather than, "no, it's too close to dinner."

176 ♥ If it feels comfortable and right, it probably is; if it doesn't feel comfortable and right, don't do it.

♥ Love, Life, and Chocolate Chip Cookies ♥

177 ♥ Children love their parents and can forgive them no matter how unfair or human parents act, and parents can profit from their children's good example by being more tolerant of children when they fail.

♥ Love, Life, and Chocolate Chip Cookies ♥

178 ♥ Children are usually the first to realize when they've done something wrong and don't need to have it pounded into them with spanking.

179 ♥ It's usually wise for moms to trust their instincts.

180 ♥ Assume children will behave in a proper manner and they usually will.

181 ♥ What we *think* we see might not be what we're *actually* seeing.

182 ♥ No one said life was fair, but parents were given brains, instincts, and common sense to protect themselves and their children.

183 ♥ Let kids solve their own problems whenever possible. It's good training for them now and important preparation for their future.

184 ♥ Forgiveness is routine when people are allowed to make their own mistakes and profit by them.

♥ LOVE, LIFE, AND CHOCOLATE CHIP COOKIES ♥

185 ♥ Children don't need to constantly prove their worth, or ever, for that matter.

♥ Love, Life, and Chocolate Chip Cookies ♥

186 ♥ One of the best things that can happen to a kid is living next door to a best friend.

187 ♥ One fourteen-year-old's comment: Moms are like horoscopes that always come true.

188 ♥ Out of the mouths of babes quite regularly come gems of wisdom.

♥ LOVE, LIFE, AND CHOCOLATE CHIP COOKIES ♥

189 ♥ Parents won't always be around to tell their children what to do or to see that they're entertained.

190 ♥ Kids often aren't allowed enough unprogrammed time. Parents seem afraid to let children get bored occasionally, yet boredom is often the springboard of creativity.

♥ Love, Life, and Chocolate Chip Cookies ♥

191 ♥ Children should have the opportunity while they're young, to learn how to make good use of spare time so it becomes a lifetime habit.

192 ♥ During early years of grade school, adulthood appears to be a distant and unrealistic goal to children.

193 ♥ Children demand freedom for enough leisure time so they can nag parents about what to do with it.

194 ♥ Any talent children can be encouraged to use and develop will grow and add to their self-esteem and sense of fulfillment, to say nothing about their own enjoyment.

♥ Love, Life, and Chocolate Chip Cookies ♥

195 ♥ Some parents may be able to help their children with homework, but are smart enough not to. Given the responsibility of doing their own work, most children will rise to the occasion.

196 ♥ With newborn teenagers around, parents should plan to hibernate their mouths for the next three to six years.

♥ LOVE, LIFE, AND CHOCOLATE CHIP COOKIES ♥

197 ♦ When adults come home from a day at the office, they're called workaholics if they bring work with them. Experts recognize the need for adults to relax and unwind. How much more do children need to "leave work at the office?"

♥ LOVE, LIFE, AND CHOCOLATE CHIP COOKIES ♥

198 ♥ Fear not, teen life, too, shall pass. But before it does, a parent's ego will be operated on and dissected into oblivion. Parents need to find a sympathetic peer group of their own to salvage any shred of sanity they have left.

199 ♥ Children judge themselves by the standards of their peers; they see themselves as either measuring up or not measuring up.

♥ Love, Life, and Chocolate Chip Cookies ♥

200 ♥ There's no satisfaction like the one we achieve after struggling to fulfill our impossible dream and succeeding.

201 ♥ It's usually during trying teen years that parents wish for their teenagers, children of their own, someday, in the teen's own image and likeness. (Do you suppose our parents wished that for us?)

202 ♥ Why is it children play nicely when there's an even number, and invariably start fighting when there's an odd number?

203 ♥ If we can all live at peace in our families, neighborhoods, and communities, maybe then we'll be able to live at peace in our world.

♥ LOVE, LIFE, AND CHOCOLATE CHIP COOKIES ♥

204 ♥ Children shown fairness and kindness are usually fair and kind; and sometimes those treated unfairly and unkindly learn compassion, rather than how to be unfair and unkind.

205 ♥ When trouble is caused by thought*less*ness, thoughtf*ull*ness may be the solution.

♥ Love, Life, and Chocolate Chip Cookies ♥

206 ♥ Senior high schoolers usually regard themselves as the repository of all knowledge. As one stupid parent to another, I say go with it! Outsmart them, but let them think they're getting their way!

207 ♥ Parents do children a disservice when they allow them to shift for themselves. Whether it's money matters, discipline, work habits, or leisure activities, children need guidance and supervision.

♥ Love, Life, and Chocolate Chip Cookies ♥

208 ♥ Parents need to give children a strong foundation, because soon enough, children have to trust their own judgment, manage themselves, and make good use of their time and money.

209 ♥ Explaining a new dent in the family car is an opportunity for a person's most creative storytelling and best acting performance.

210 ♥ Preach to your kids for years, tell them how to behave, and occasionally you might get through to them. Be a good example, however, and they'll never forget the lesson.

211 ♥ A good example children must see is their parents picking themselves up after failing, then trying a little harder until they succeed.

212 ♥ If you want good children, be a good parent.

213 ♥ People who repress and nurture anger are people who hold grudges and lose all capability to forgive.

214 ♥ Children learn how to make wise decisions when they're judged wisely.

215 ♥ Parents who always shelter children from hard times may be doing them a disservice. Caring and sharing parents should help children realize that hard times will pass, just as they did for mom and dad.

216 ♥ When justice is left to the Lord, we don't have to bother with it ourselves, therefore, simplifying our lives.

217 ♥ By walking away from and forgetting a bad incident, a person minimizes its importance and limits its influence.

218 ♥ Much of how teenagers behave goes back to their childhood and how much they respected their parents, if their parents were even around to earn respect.

♥ LOVE, LIFE, AND CHOCOLATE CHIP COOKIES ♥

219 ♥ Without suffering through the lows that come to us, we can't fully appreciate the highs that follow.

220 ♥ Parents need to keep lines of communication open, striving to talk *with* their children rather than *at* them.

221 ♥ Bad behavior by a child in senior high may simply be a means of trying to reduce or compensate for the anticipated pain of leaving home. It's the child's defense mechanism against sorrow.

222 ♥ How a parent asks a question usually determines what gets done.

♥ Love, Life, and Chocolate Chip Cookies ♥

223 ♥ A parent's bad memory sometimes makes parenting easier.

224 ♥ There are unusual events in each of our lives, but the memorable ones are sometimes so humble, we wonder why we remember them so well after so many years.

♥ LOVE, LIFE, AND CHOCOLATE CHIP COOKIES ♥

225 ♥ Family gatherings can be well planned, spontaneous, gourmet, or fast food. What's important is family being reunited.

226 ♥ Families aren't whipping posts for our problems of the day, but precious gifts to love, nourish, and cherish.

227 ♥ Teenagers may fight family rules, but they secretly prefer direction.

228 ♥ The world has made it difficult for children to be independent. Parents should be loving, patient, and understanding, but they needn't be floor mats!

♥ Love, Life, and Chocolate Chip Cookies ♥

229 ♥ When parents and young adult children can't seem to get together on rules, it might be time for the young adults to move out. No disgrace to that.

230 ♥ A woman's best friends are other women.

231 ♥ Women teach each other to laugh as they realize there are no unique problems.

232 ♥ Women help each other save a few marriages, heal a few wounds, or encourage each other to laugh at problems.

233 ♥ Only one thing mars the joy of the empty nest syndrome: kids moving back home once they've left.

♥ Love, Life, and Chocolate Chip Cookies ♥

234 ♥ There's so much beauty for our mind to take in, we shouldn't clutter it with garbage.

235 ♥ Perfectionists are usually people who expect perfection in everyone but themselves.

236 ♥ Walking clears the head, stimulates the body, and feeds the soul through the eyes.

♥ Love, Life, and Chocolate Chip Cookies ♥

237 ♥ Take your children for a walk so you can discover God's gifts together.

238 ♥ When we look around us and see kindness in friends and neighbors, it's hard to understand how there can be so much evil in the world.

♥ Love, Life, and Chocolate Chip Cookies ♥

239 ♥ Too bad we don't iron any more; it was such good thinking time.

240 ♥ People who practice justice are usually a source of embarrassment to their families.

241 ♥ Parenthood is a privilege.

♥ Love, Life, and Chocolate Chip Cookies ♥

242 ♥ Kneel to reach a child and grow in stature.

243 ♥ If doing good makes us feel that way, how can we ever do evil?

244 ♥ Money isn't evil, only the abuse of it is.

245 ♥ Be comfortable with yourself.

♥ Love, Life, and Chocolate Chip Cookies ♥

246 ♥ We need to treat ourselves at least once a week.

247 ♥ The root of all evil isn't money, but the lack of it.

248 ♥ Happiness is quiet time alone in the morning to begin our day, and again in the evening to end it.

♥ Love, Life, and Chocolate Chip Cookies ♥

249 ♥ In spring we smell lilac in bloom, freshly cut grass, rain in the air, and a field of freshly plowed earth...we need never despair.

250 ♥ Leaves begin with an illusion of green in early spring. In summer they shield us from the sun's heat and, before they die, put on the most magnificent show of their short lives.

♥ LOVE, LIFE, AND CHOCOLATE CHIP COOKIES ♥

251 ♥ Consistency of nature reassures us.

252 ♥ What fun to watch our children blossom into unique individuals discovering their talents.

253 ♥ There's nothing like the feel of well kneaded bread under our palms.

♥ Love, Life, and Chocolate Chip Cookies ♥

254 ♥ Teach children they always have a direct line to God, because God is within and around them.

255 ♥ Divide the purchase price by your hourly pay rate, calculate how many hours you have to work to pay for it, and discover how easy it becomes to separate the necessary from the things you can go without.

256 ♥ Glance around any casino and decide who looks like the winner: the casino or you, then act accordingly.

257 ♥ Flowers grow in fertile soil, ideas in fertile brains.

258 ♥ Sometimes the richest people we meet in life are the poorest financially.

♥ LOVE, LIFE, AND CHOCOLATE CHIP COOKIES ♥

259 ♥ Christ threw moneychangers out of the temple; we honor them.

260 ♥ Wings that were tightly compressed against my sides have opened of their own accord and refuse to be put back into their cocoon.

261 ♥ Tea parties are for everyone.

♥ Love, Life, and Chocolate Chip Cookies ♥

262 ♥ Marriage isn't for everyone, but some discover it too late.

263 ♥ Becoming one with another person doesn't mean giving up our individuality; rather, it grows and blossoms with encouragement.

264 ♥ Petty people are self- important.

♥ Love, Life, and Chocolate Chip Cookies ♥

265 ♥ A successful marriage learns to distinguish the trivial from the important, and ignore the trivial.

266 ♥ Little people talk about themselves; great people are talked about by others.

267 ♥ Children should be the only little people.

268 ♥ Justice, love, and good humor should be so much a part of our character, we never have to consciously think about them.

269 ♥ We cast judgment on ourselves everytime we open our mouths.

270 ♥ In a perfect world, our mate would be our best friend.

♥ Love, Life, and Chocolate Chip Cookies ♥

271 ♥ Playing together encourages staying together.

272 ♥ It's ideal when love and marriage go together.

273 ♥ Facts are quite often the opposite of what they appear.

♥ Love, Life, and Chocolate Chip Cookies ♥

274 ♥ A sale is a bargain only if you needed the item in the first place.

275 ♥ A bad temper should be kept to ourself, because most certainly no one else wants it.

276 ♥ We owe everyone the dignity of a polite reply.

♥ Love, Life, and Chocolate Chip Cookies ♥

277 ♥ Family deserves at least the same courtesy we give strangers.

278 ♥ Sticks and stones may break our bones, but cruel words hurt even worse.

279 ♥ Parents without honor in their own homes have failed.

♥ Love, Life, and Chocolate Chip Cookies ♥

280 ♥ Bad days teach us more about life than good days.

281 ♥ Just causes often lose, but those who fight for them don't.

282 ♥ Fair treatment teaches more than a book on the subject.

♥ Love, Life, and Chocolate Chip Cookies ♥

283 ♥ Life should be a labor of love.

284 ♥ Be honest and fair, and people will find you.

285 ♥ Parents working cheerfully alongside their children on household jobs, teach a valuable lesson.

286 ♥ The lace and fluff of our wedding day have taken new form; we're muslin and denim, mended, remended, and patched.

287 ♥ Parents must set a good example for children, but when they fail, another good example for kids is hearing parents admit their error, and seeing them trying to do better. No one is perfect all the time; kids need to see that.

288 ♥ Be taking the last of the chocolate chip cookies out of the oven when the kids get home from school. They'll smell them halfway down the block and burst in the door with happy smiles on their faces; cookies for them, hugs for mom!

ALSO FROM ST. JOHN'S PUBLISHING . . .

• • •

Parenting a Business, by Donna L. Montgomery, looks at business relationships from a parenting standpoint.

Surviving Motherhood, by Donna L. Montgomery. A look at family relationships written by a mother of eight who is a survivor of motherhood herself.

Kids+ Modeling= Money, by Donna L. Montgomery, is all you need to help your child begin a rewarding and prosperous modeling career. Discover the secrets of modeling success.

• • •

St. John's Publishing
6824 Oaklawn Avenue
Edina, MN 55435

Please send me _____ copy (copies) of **Parenting a Business** (ISBN 0-938577-04-2). I am enclosing $14.95 and $1.50 for shipping for each copy.

Please send me _____ copy (copies) of **Surviving Motherhood**, (ISBN 0-938577-00-X). I am enclosing $6.95 and $1.50 for shipping for each copy.

Please send me _____ copy (copies) of **Kids+ Modeling= Money,** (ISBN 0-13-515172-4). I am enclosing $9.95 (hardcover) and $1.50 for shipping for each copy.

NAME _____

ADDRESS _____

_____

_____

_____